DON'T ROCK THE BOAT!

THE STORY OF THE MIRACULOUS CATCH

By Marilyn Lashbrook

Illustrated by Stephanie McFetridge Britt

candle
BOOKS

Catching fish is man's work; catching men is God's work. Jesus showed his disciples how to do both. "Don't Rock the Boat" will assure your child that God has the power to care for him and to help him do great things.

Pretending is a fun way for children to learn. Pause after questions and commands to allow your child to act out rowing, tossing and pulling in fish nets and sitting very still.

If it's bed time, act out the closing poem — following you to the kitchen for a drink, to the bathroom to brush teeth and to bed for prayer and sleep.

First published in the UK by Candle Books Ltd. 1994. Distributed by STL., P.O. Box 300, Carlisle, Cumbria CA3 0JH.

Coedition arranged by Angus Hudson Ltd., London.

Printed in Italy.

ISBN 0 948902 92 2

Don't Rock The Boat!

THE STORY OF THE MIRACULOUS CATCH

By Marilyn Lashbrook

Illustrated by Stephanie McFetridge Britt

Taken from Luke 5

Peter and his friends
had fished all night long,
but they hadn't caught a single fish.

As they rowed their boats to shore,
the colours of the morning sky
dancced on the water.

But Peter, James, and John
did not care about the sunrise.
They were tired and grumpy.

(Can you make a grumpy face?)

They climbed out of the boats
and tossed their nets into the water.
It was time to wash
the slippery, slimy seaweed
out of the nets.

*(Can you pretend
you are washing fish nets?)*

Peter spread his nets on the sand
and waited for them to dry.
He was very unhappy
about not catching fish.
He always caught fish!

Then Peter heard someone coming.
He looked up.
There was the Lord Jesus.

Jesus asked Peter to take Him
for a ride in his boat,
and Peter gladly did.

"Throw in your nets," said Jesus.
Peter was surprised!
"We fished all night," he complained,
"and we didn't catch a thing.
But if you say so..."

And Peter obeyed.
Would you like to pretend
you are Peter throwing the net?

As soon as the net hit the water,
it was filled with
lots and lots of wiggly fish.

"Hurry!" Peter yelled,
"Bring the other boat!"

James and John jumped into their boat
and rowed as fast as they could!
Splish-splash, splish-splash, splish-splash!

Peter and his friends
tugged and tugged.

(Can you help pull in the nets?)

"Oh, these fish are
so heavy!" they laughed.
Now, they were very happy!

The men pulled in so many fish
that their boats could barely float!

(Sit very still! Don't rock the boat!)

Peter and his friends
rowed s-l-o-w-l-y back to shore.
They had NEVER had a catch
like this before.

Peter was amazed.
Only God could have brought
that many fish into their nets.
It was wonderful
to go fishing with Jesus!

But Jesus told him
there was something better
than catching a lot of fish.

"Follow me," Jesus said.
"I will make you fishers of men."

Peter, James and John
left their nets
and followed Jesus.

We want to fish for men.
  (clap, clap)
And save them out of sin.
  (clap, clap)
We'll talk of God's love,
And Heaven above.
We want to fish for men.
  (clap, clap)

ME TOO!
B O O K S

For Ages 2-5

SOMEONE TO LOVE
THE STORY OF CREATION

TWO BY TWO
THE STORY OF NOAH'S FAITH

"I DON'T WANT TO"
THE STORY OF JONAH

"I MAY BE LITTLE"
THE STORY OF DAVID'S GROWTH

"I'LL PRAY ANYWAY"
THE STORY OF DANIEL

WHO NEEDS A BOAT?
THE STORY OF MOSES

"GET LOST LITTLE BROTHER"
THE STORY OF JOSEPH

THE WALL THAT DID NOT FALL
THE STORY OF RAHAB'S FAITH

NO TREE FOR CHRISTMAS
THE STORY OF JESUS' BIRTH

"NOW I SEE"
THE STORY OF THE MAN BORN BLIND

DON'T ROCK THE BOAT!
THE STORY OF THE MIRACULOUS CATCH

OUT ON A LIMB
THE STORY OF ZACCHAEUS